THE EVERYBODY GETS ANXIOUS ACTIVITY BOOK

JORDAN REID · ERIN WILLIAMS

RODALE KIDS NEW YORK

For Lucy, River, and Shea — J.R. & E.W.

Text copyright © 2022 by Jordan Reid and Erin Williams
Cover art and interior illustrations copyright © 2022 by Erin Williams

All rights reserved. Published in the United States by Rodale Kids, an imprint of
Random House Children's Books, a division of Penguin Random House LLC, New York.

Rodale and the colophon are registered trademarks and Rodale Kids
is a trademark of Penguin Random House LLC.

Visit us on the Web! rhcbooks.com

Educators and librarians, for a variety of teaching tools, visit us at RHTeachersLibrarians.com

Library of Congress Cataloging-in-Publication Data is available upon request.
ISBN 978-0-593-43380-5 (trade)

The artist used digital tools to create the illustrations for this book.
Interior design by Erin Williams

MANUFACTURED IN CHINA
10 9 8 7 6 5 4 3 2 1
First Edition

HELLO THERE!

WELCOME to your new activity book. I'm Chesterfield B. Wigglesworth, Anxiety Monster in Residence, but everyone calls me Wigs. Maybe it's because of my impossibly shiny, wonderfully luxurious fur. Not totally sure on that one.

Hi my name is.. **Wigs!!**

But enough about me. **YOU'RE HERE!** And YOU are just who I wanted to see. Sit down and snuggle up. Or stand up and run in circles around your bedroom. Or do jumping jacks while balancing your collection of fidget spinners on your head. Whatever makes you happy!

Consider this book your personal **WIGOUT ZONE**, where you get to shower me with as many gifts and as much praise as you possibly can. I also like snacks.

⚠ ALERT!! ⚠

We interrupt this message to bring you an important note from the authors of this book:

While we welcome Mr. Wigglesworth's opinions, his job is to be your friendly guide through the ups, downs, highs, lows, and epic swings of your anxious feelings.

OFFICIAL CONTRACT

I will be a friendly guide through the ups, downs, highs, lows, and epic swings of kids' anxious feelings. I will not get presents or snacks.

Signed,
Christopher B. Wigglesworth

SIGH. Fiiiine. As I was saying, it's my job to help you get comfy with your feelings, get some ideas for how to handle them, and—most importantly— HAVE FUN.

HOW TO USE THIS BOOK

If you get hungry, page 72 looks yummy...

1. Do you have a pen? A pencil? A feathered quill that you time-warped in from the 16th century? A tiny piece of crayon that you found in the creepy spot between your bed and the wall? You're ready to start!

2. Pick up this book whenever you feel like it: in the morning, because it's more fun to do activities than to wonder whether that quiz is scheduled for today or tomorrow (it's tomorrow . . . right?); during lunch, instead of being annoyed that Alex always manages to sit in the spot you were just about to sit in (how do they even do that?); or just before bed, so you can get ready for tonight's excellent dream.

3. This book technically has a beginning, a middle, and an end, but you can totally ignore that fact, because activity books aren't really the kind of thing you have to do in order. Flip forward, flip backward, head straight to the middle to say hi to Shush the Tiny Worry Monster: Whatever you want! You don't even have to finish this book if you don't want to! You get an A+ no matter what.

WHAT IS ANXIETY?

Anxiety is our body's 100% normal response to finding itself in a stressful situation.

Who, me?

Maybe your anxiety shows up as fear, or as nervousness, or even as a stomachache! It has a lot of disguises it likes to use.

Some anxieties are really common. For example, taking a test makes most people feel jittery. Other anxieties are pretty rare, but that doesn't mean they're not real.

On the rare side, famous psychologist Sigmund Freud was deathly afriad of ferns.

Anxiety is also pretty good at hiding. Even if someone you know seems like they never get worried, remember: They may just be holding their anxiety somewhere deep inside. Everybody has anxiety, but anxiety looks different for everyone.

HOW SENSITIVE IS YOUR SMOKE ALARM?

THE BIG QUESTION:

When does anxiety become a problem?

When our anxieties start taking over so much space in our brain that there's not much room for good feelings, it's a smart idea to look for tools to help us manage them.

Lots of anxiety experts suggest that you think of your anxiety as a smoke alarm. It's important to have a smoke alarm in your house because it can save your life in a fire. But what if your smoke alarm started going off when there was no real danger?

BBRRRINGG

BEEP
BEEP
BEEP

Your smoke alarm is helpful—even essential!—when it's working correctly, but if it starts going off all the time over a little burned toast, you'll *probably* want to do something about it. After all, that much noise can make it hard to think straight.

It's the same with anxiety: It can help us figure out when we're in actual danger, which is great! If it starts showing up all over the place when it doesn't really need to, though, we might end up avoiding cool opportunities or fun adventures.

It's just toast.

FOOD FOR THOUGHT:

How sensitive is your smoke alarm?

If your smoke alarm rang a little less often, what might you be able to do?

QUIZ TIME!

Let's take a quick quiz to find out more about you and your feelings. Check all that apply!

On an average day, I feel anxious:
- [ ] Eh, not much
- [ ] When something happens that I wasn't expecting
- [ ] When I can't think of anything to do
- [ ] When I have too many things to do
- [ ] When my sibling does this thing that makes me CRAZY: _____
- [ ] When I haven't gotten a good night's sleep
- [ ] When I feel like nobody is listening to me
- [ ] Um, always?

Things that are currently making me anxious:
- [ ] School
- [ ] Doing the dishes
- [ ] My sibling(s)
- [ ] Bullies
- [ ] Peer pressure
- [ ] Fitting in
- [ ] Vegetables
- [ ] Sharks
- [ ] Wondering whether I'm going to get onto this team: _____
- [ ] The fact that insects exist and there are really a lot of them out there
- [ ] All of the above, plus everything else, UGH

I know I'm feeling anxious when I:
☐ Can't fall asleep no matter what I try
☐ Get mad really easily, or for reasons that usually wouldn't bother me
☐ Don't want to talk, at all, to anyone
☐ Cry a lot more easily than usual
☐ Feel like my face is really hot
☐ Sweat a bunch
☐ Get a stomachache
☐ Can't stop thinking about a problem even if it's one I can't solve

I'd feel much more anxious right now if I were:
☐ Standing alone in front of my class
☐ Starting my first day at a new school
☐ At the doctor's office
☐ About to play kickball
☐ Taking a test
☐ At sleepaway camp
☐ Doing this very specific thing that only I understand is
  The Actual Worst: _____

This is how good I am at handling my anxiety:
☐ Does curling up in a ball count as "handling it"?
☐ It feels pretty overwhelming most of the time
☐ I can usually work through it with some techniques I've learned
☐ I'm basically Yoda

I've had to ask for help with my anxiety, too!

DO YOU NEED ANSWERS?

All of these reactions are normal. Common, even! But remember the smoke alarm: If yours is going off so much that it's interfering with your day-to-day activities, it's time to ask for help.

TOP 5 FEARS THAT TOTALLY MAKE SENSE

Orange juice pulp

1.

2.

3.

4.

5.

Suddenly not wearing pants

Aunt Margo's famous casserole

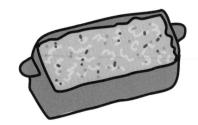

Skunks

Murder hornets

WHAT IS THIS KID AFRAID OF?

What would you say to help them feel less scared?

_____

_____

_____

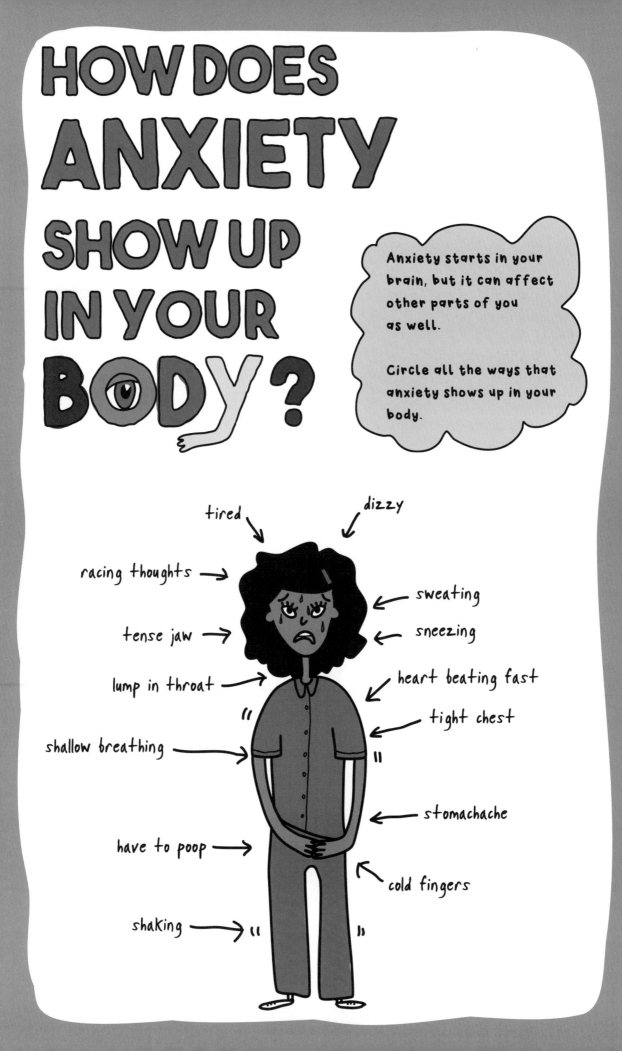

worry BINGO

Put a coin (or a chocolate chip, or an X) on all the things that have made you anxious. If you fill an entire row, congratulations! You made it through, and also you deserve a cookie.

Too much homework	Lunch so gross	Late for the bus	Booooored	Pet doesn't want petting
Called on by teacher	Not called on by teacher	Argument with friend	Rain	P.E. class
Skinned knee	Peas for dinner	free space!	Moving	Hangnail
Saw a wasp	Sibling so annoying	Ugh so tired	Lost homework	Eek, the dentist
New pimple	Got a shot	What's that smell?	Bad dream	Felt sick

A DAY IN THE LIFE OF MY FEELINGS

Every day has its sunny and stormy spots. Some days are sunnier (or stormier) than others, but the weather always changes eventually.

What's your weather forecast today? _____

Now let's see if your forecast comes true! Fill in the weather symbol that best represents your feelings at each point today.

8:00 am:

10:00 am:

12:00 pm:

2:00 pm:

4:00 pm:

6:00 pm:

8:00 pm:

Bedtime:

Key:

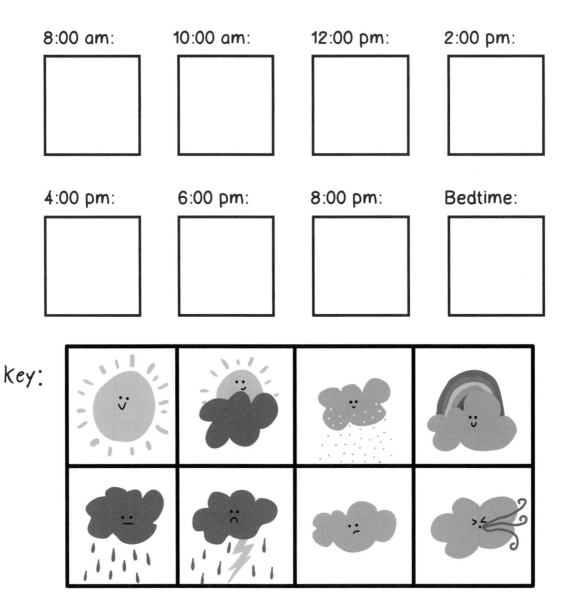

DRAW WHAT YOU USE TO GET OUT OF THE RAIN

the FIGHT, FLIGHT, OR FREEZE RESPONSE: A VERY HELPFUL THING (SOMETIMES)

Ever noticed that when you get really, really upset, you sometimes find that you want to run away? Or stomp and yell? Or maybe your mind goes completely blank, and you feel like you're glued to the floor?

Here's the interesting part: This reaction is an instinct. It actually helped keep the human species alive!

Let's go back a couple hundred thousand years.

Nowadays, we're much less likely to come across a bear or tiger out in the wild, but our minds don't always realize that. Sometimes they tell our bodies to react to even small worries as if they're big scary beasts that might hurt us, instead of what they actually are.

So next time you find yourself wanting to fight, fly, or freeze, remember: Anxiety might be trying to get you to run back into your cave, but it's not the boss of you.

You are.

MORE WAYS YOUR ANXIETY COMES IN HANDY!

It makes you much better prepared for alien invasions.

Anxiety can make you feel more alert and focused. It's basically like accessing your secret superpowers.

If you see a rabid hyena, you are very unlikely to try to pet it. This is an excellent decision.

Draw your own!

GET TO YOUR LUNCH TABLE WITH ZERO DISASTERS!

Avoid moldy tater tots! Spilled chocolate milk! Cafeteria supervisors who always think you're doing something wrong when, excuse me, you're totally not!

← Go!

You did it!

COLOR IN THE THINGS THAT ARE SERIOUSLY UNLIKELY TO HAPPEN

Drowning in a vat of M&M's

Fall into toilet and get stuck forever

Must wrestle The Rock

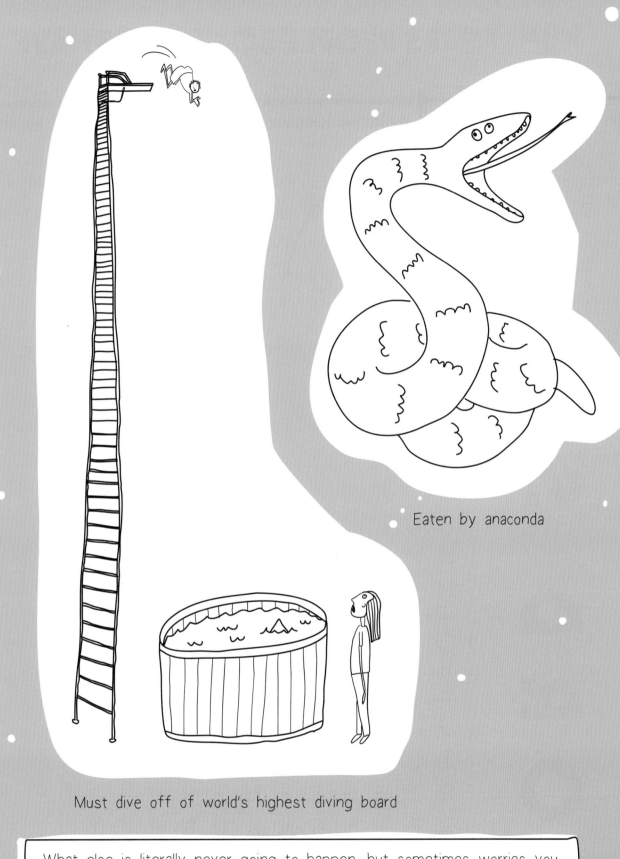

Eaten by anaconda

Must dive off of world's highest diving board

What else is literally never going to happen, but sometimes worries you anyway?

_____

_____

WORD SEARCH

FEARS PEOPLE SOMETIMES HAVE

Find the (very) common fears that (lots of) people have.

The dark   Centipedes   Crowds
Heights   Blood   Being alone
Mummies   Ghosts   Baby animals

```
M C X N Z Z C N A D B Z
U U E N C R S T S O H G
M K N N O S K Q X E X W
M M C W T R F I V P Z L
I D D U A I T G T S Y C
E S O D L S P N M X D P
S J E O Z O P E V B V K
U H I J L K Z P D X M T
T E I C D B P J E E I E
S T H G I E H H R V S Y
B E I N G A L O N E T F
B A B Y A N I M A L S D
```

Just kidding. Nobody is scared of baby animals.

FEELINGS RAINBOW

Scientists have found that colors have the ability to spark emotions in people. But not necessarily the same emotions—blue, for example, might feel peaceful to you, but your best friend might think of it as a sad color. Circle the word that describes how each color feels like to you. Then color in the rainbow of feelings.

Mysterious
Magical
Sensitive

Peaceful
Sad
Trustworthy

Kind
Curious
Balanced

Powerful
Angry
Passionate

Adventurous
Brave
Cheerful

Creative
Happy
Strong

DRAW FACES ON THESE UNDERWATER CREATURES, WHO ARE FEELING LOTS OF THINGS

Tired turtle

Successful swordfish

Smug seahorse

Frustrated fish

Worried whale

Mad manta ray

Confident crab

Optimistic octopus

REVEAL THE SECRETS OF YOUR MIND!

You know the thing that just popped into your head? Yeah, that thing. Draw it!

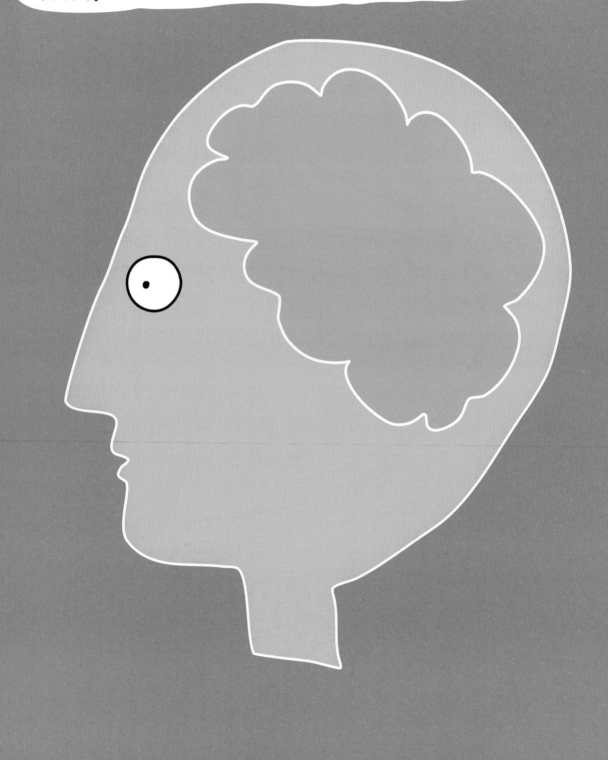

WHY BEING A NERD IS SO COOL

Some people think that being branded a nerd is the worst thing in the world. Um, please. First of all, who gets to decide what's "cool" and what's "dorky"? (Spoiler alert: you do.)

Some reasons to wear that Nerd Badge with pride:

American hero Katherine Johnson

From Steve Wozniak (who invented the first Apple computer in his garage) to Katherine Johnson (whose work at NASA put humans on the moon), nerds have been behind many of the world's biggest and most important discoveries. Basically, nerds rule the world.

Kindness is a muscle!

If you're teased for some so-called "nerdy" ways, know that it'll make you stronger (because tough situations help you grow) and kinder (because you'll learn that words can hurt—and you won't use your own words to hurt another).

And finally: Being a nerd means never having to play it cool, so if you're excited about something, you get to just . . . be excited. How great is that?!

DO SOMETHING NICE

Guaranteed way to make yourself feel better: Do something nice for another person. Works every time.

A few ideas:

1. Do a chore that's usually someone else's responsibility.
2. Donate a bag of your old clothes to charity.
3. Sing Christmas carols to your neighbors in July.
4. Give one of your favorite books to a friend who'll love it, too.
5. Write a thank-you note to your mail carrier or garbage collector.
6. Give your old toys to a younger neighbor.
7. Hold the door open for someone.
8. Scatter heads-up pennies in your neighborhood.
9. Write a letter to a family member telling them why you love them.
10. Plant a tree.
11. Rescue a worm.
12. Call an older relative and ask them questions about their childhood. Stay on the phone as long as they want.
13. Be nice to your sibling for an ENTIRE DAY.
14. Give a friend a sincere compliment.
15. At lunchtime, sit next to someone who might want company.
16. Take out a neighbor's trash.
17. Clean your room without being asked.
18. Kiss a frog.
19. Offer someone else your seat.
20. Give a hug to a person who needs one.

TOP THIS Giant CUPCAKE!

Suggested toppings

- Frosting
- Additional frosting
- A cherry
- Sprinkles
- Extra more lotsa frosting
- Ice cream
- Elves
- Chocolate drizzle
- Whipped cream
- Caramel sauce
- Peanut butter

Elf for scale

MAKE YOUR OWN MINI-COMIC!

INSTRUCTIONS:

Step 1: Use the box over here →
to write about a time that you were scared and how you overcame that fear.

Step 2: Grab a pencil and sketch out your comic on the opposite page.

Step 3: To finish, ink* and color your comic!

*Trace over the lines using pen

Um, feel free to improve the title?

That Time I Was Scared and Then Not Scared

By

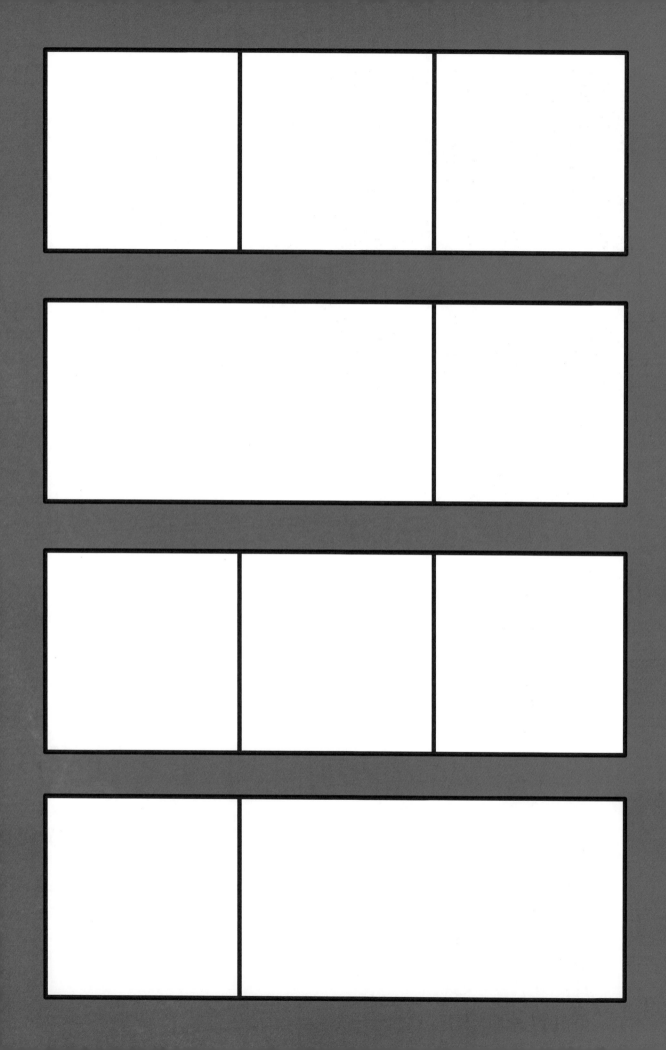

FEARS THAT YOU KNOW DON'T MAKE SENSE, BUT STILL

Clowns, yikes

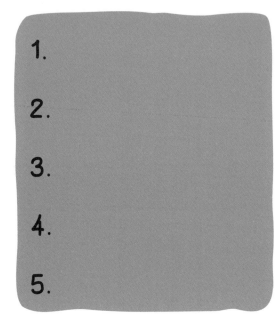

Spiders that only live in faraway jungles

Getting only broccoli for dinner forever

1.

2.

3.

4.

5.

Being sent to Greenland to live with a gnome family

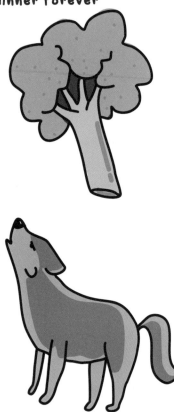

Being eaten by wolves

TRASH *your* FEARS

Draw those five things that scare you being chucked into this flaming dumpster. See ya!

PRESENTATION TIME!

!!!

Standing up in front of the entire class can be super stressful, but did you know that most people (like 75%!) get freaked out by the idea of public speaking?

that's a lot

Here are a few easy things you can do to calm your nerves.

ADMIT THAT YOU'RE NERVOUS

don't do this →

I am fine.

"   "

Fears hate being talked about. It makes them want to run far, far away.

PRETEND YOU'RE BLOWING UP A BIG BALLOON

Sometimes when we get nervous we actually forget to breathe. Not breathing is a terrible idea. Take big, deep breaths in through the nose and out through the mouth.

OOF

STAND WITH EQUAL WEIGHT ON BOTH FEET

It instantly makes you feel more confident.

½   ½

PICTURE YOURSELF BEING AMAZING

You're standing on a mountaintop! You just won the battle that saved the world from all the bad guys (yes, all of them)! You are basically an Avenger!

you get a medal!

GET REAL

Remember that most of the kids in your class are probably wondering whether there's pizza for lunch, or thinking about llamas.

aww...

WHAT'S EVERYONE IN CLASS THINKING?

QUESTIONS EVERYONE ASKS THEMSELVES WHILE WAITING FOR CLASS TO END

When is recess?

When is lunch?

When is the next holiday where I get a present?

What's for lunch?

Is that clock broken? It's definitely broken.

Are giraffes actually supposed to look like that, or was it an accident?

Why can't scientists make spinach taste like Cheetos?

When someone farts near you and you smell it, does that mean you're breathing in little bits of poop?

Why is lunch so far away?

I'm hungry.

Me too.

NOW FILL THIS LUNCH BOX WITH YOUR ABSOLUTE MOST PERFECTEST LUNCH

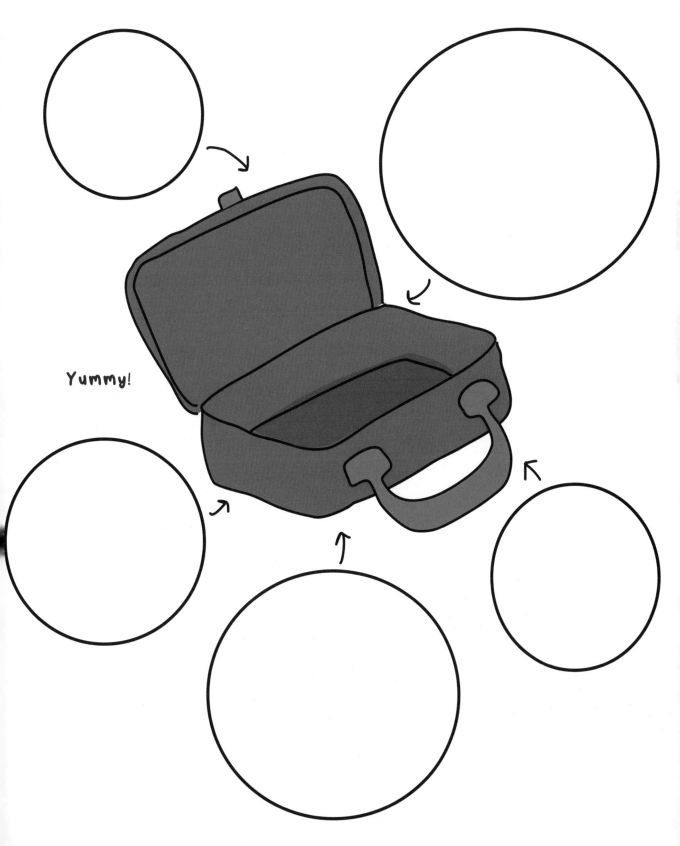

Yummy!

WORD SEARCH

2020

Were you alive in the year 2020? Then you never, ever want to hear these words again.

COVID
Quarantine

Pod
Unmute

Zoom
Toilet paper

```
Q R R G Q U B T I S I N
H L D K D N S R B D C C
C X I I Z M J E E G O E
D S V V I U C P S X S F
S O E N I T N A R A U Q
C G Z Y U E Z P Q Y P V
H Y Z O O M E T J K A M
B Z N V G C T E N L F X
Q N H O L G E L H A L O
P N S P F B E I I Q U T
L J O F K B A O A W H N
A D X Z O W I T F K L B
```

COMPLETE *the* STORY:
THE FIRST DAY OF SCHOOL

It was a/n _____ morning. I woke up at _____
                Adjective   Tme of day

and got out of my _____ . I put on a/n _____ ,
                        Noun   Item of clothing

then ate some _____ . I was feeling pretty _____ .
                     Food   Emotion

I was hoping that I'd get _____ for homeroom!
                              Adult's name

     When I got to school, the first person I saw was _____ .
                                                          Person

"_____ ," they said. "Wow, that's a cool _____
        Greeting   Noun

you're carrying!" I said. We walked into the _____ —it
                                            Place

was full of _____ and _____ , and everyone was
               Plural noun   Plural noun

_____ .
Verb ending in -ing

     It turned out I got _____ for homeroom! I was so
                               Adult's name

_____ . They taught us all about _____ —the
     Emotion   Plural noun

lesson took _____ so by the end I was super _____ .
              Amount of time   Adjective

At lunch, I ate _____ and drank _____ . Yum! Then
                  Food   Drink

it was time for recess, where I played _____ with a
                                    Game

_____ . When the last bell rang, I grabbed my _____
     Noun   Noun

and headed to _____ so I could _____ .
               Place   Verb

     Overall, it was a pretty _____ first day. I'll give it a
                                     Adjective

_____ .
Grade

LET'S SOLVE SOME PROBLEMS!

I am the ghost of George Washington and I approve this quiz.

Boo!

Choose the correct way to handle each tricky situation.

You're invited to a party, but you don't think you'll know many people there. Do you:
   a) Write the host a note saying "Parties are stupid and so are you"?
   b) Say you came down with a sudden case of mortificidus* and hide under your blankets all night?
   c) Decide that you'll go—and you'll just climb out the bathroom window if no one talks to you?
   d) Ask if it'd be okay if you bring a friend along, and pledge to try talking to at least one new person?

You feel like one of your friends is upset with you, but you don't know what you did. Do you:
   a) Scream "WHY DO YOU HATE ME SO MUCH" and burst into tears?
   b) Never talk to them ever again?
   c) Ask another friend to try to figure out what's wrong, and then report back to you?
   d) Say "Hey, I feel like you might be upset with me. Is there anything you want to talk about?"

*This is not a thing.

You shared a secret you'd promised your friend you'd keep, and they're really embarrassed. Do you:
- a) Say "The ghost of George Washington made me do it"?
- b) Collapse on the ground and cry until everyone feels even worse for you than they do for your friend?
- c) Tell your friend that you hate to be the one to tell them, but it was totally your other friend who did it?
- d) Apologize sincerely and promise not to make that mistake again?

You tripped on a step walking into school and fell flat on your face in front of EVERYONE. Do you:
- a) Play dead?
- b) Get up and do it over and over and over again so everybody thinks it's a comedy routine?
- c) Go directly to the nurse's office and stay there for the next 5 to 10 years?
- d) Laugh it off, and get on with your day because hello: Everybody trips?

You forgot that your essay was due today, and didn't finish it. Do you:
- a) Run away and join the circus?
- b) Dig a big hole and crawl into it?
- c) Yell "LOOK, IT'S AN ULTRA-RARE KILLER BUTTERFLY!" to change the subject?
- d) Calmly explain the problem to your teacher and ask them for an extension?

DO YOU NEED ANSWERS?

(D) is the best choice in all of the above situations, except if your mom actually has a pet kinkajou, in which case what are you doing filling out an activity book?!?! Go play with that kinkajou, it's ADORABLE.

HOW MANY WORDS CAN YOU MAKE OUT OF THE LETTERS IN SNOW DAY?

Using just the letters above, make as many words as you can. Here, we did some for you.

Soda
_____

Sandy
_____

Wand
_____

_____

_____

_____

_____

_____

_____

_____

_____

_____

_____

_____

_____

_____

_____

_____

WORD ASSOCIATION TIME

What's the first word that pops into your mind when you read each of the below?

Dodgeball: _____

Shower: _____

Winter break: _____

Homeroom: _____

Pop quiz: _____

Circus: _____

Sick day: _____

Halloween: _____

Superhero: _____

Shoe shopping: _____

Boogers: _____

Cafeteria food: _____

The Queen of England: _____

Zoom classes: _____

Tiny, fuzzy puppies: _____

ANXIETY CHECK-IN

Hey, how ya doin'?

Today is: ___ / ___ / ___ .

On a scale of 1 (least) to 10 (most), my anxiety is a _____ today.

I'd be more anxious right now if I were:
☐ Being forced to eat anchovies
☐ At the dentist's
☐ Cleaning my room
☐ Being asked "So how was your day?"
☐ Trying to pick a wedgie in public

I'd be less anxious right now if I were:
☐ Watching my favorite movie (this one: _____)
☐ Sitting in an enormous bean bag
☐ Making s'mores over a campfire
☐ Taking a bubble bath
☐ Getting a hug

The thing that makes me feel better is:
☐ Using my genius math skills to figure out the statistical probability that a Very Bad Thing will happen
☐ Watching YouTube videos about slime
☐ Playing this sport: _____
☐ Talking to this person: _____
☐ Having a good, hard cry

The thing I'm most worried about today is _____
_____ ,
but this probably won't happen because _____
_____ .
And even if it did happen, everything would eventually be okay, because
_____
_____ .

WHEW.

FEELING STRESSED?
TAKE A NAP!

Sometimes when we feel too many uncomfortable things, all we need to feel better is a little sleep. Draw yourself taking a rest in this super-comfy bed! Or snooze IRL instead.

Can't move

Closet monster

Lions and tigers and bears

Lost a super-important thing

ASTROPHYSICS
LATIN
GIANT BUGS

Naked in class

Falling off building

RANK THESE SITUATIONS FROM YAYYYYY TO NOPE NOPE NOPE

From 1 to 6 , how do you feel about each of the below?

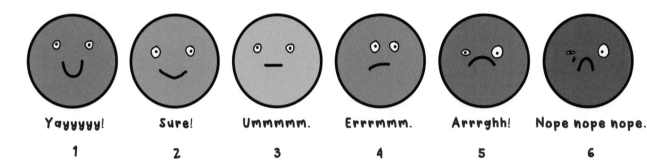

| Yayyyyy! | Sure! | Ummmmm. | Errrmmm. | Arrrghh! | Nope nope nope. |
| 1 | 2 | 3 | 4 | 5 | 6 |

_____ Learning trigonometry

_____ Favorite device broke (this one: _____)

_____ WiFi is down

_____ Bed is unmade

_____ Dirty socks

_____ Mosquito bites

_____ Eating spicy stuff

_____ Can't find the very last puzzle piece

_____ Chores

_____ Getting up super early

_____ Have to get your teeth cleaned

_____ Farted in public

_____ Have to poop at a friend's house

_____ Thunderstorms

_____ Putting on sunscreen

_____ Cafeteria meatloaf

DESIGN YOUR OWN EMOJI

...that perfectly expresses how you feel today.

SCAVENGER HUNT

FIND THE COMFORTING THINGS AROUND YOUR HOUSE

☐ Favorite book

☐ Coziest blanket

☐ Fluffiest pillow

☐ Comfy socks

Now snuggle up with your drink and your snack and read that book!

☐ Super-soft sweatshirt

☐ Drink that's just the right temperature

☐ Healthy snack

☐ Floofy pet, if available

YOU HAVE ARRIVED AT THE CENTER OF THIS BOOK

I don't get much company. I get nervous when I'm around lots of people. I like Wigs, though. He brings me cheese sometimes, and cheese is delicious. Who are some people you really like being around? Why do you like them so much?

They sound really nice.

I hope they come here someday . . . I think. Sometimes I get sweaty when I meet new people.

I haven't left this page in ages. It's scary out there in the rest of this book. I might get lost in a maze, or trapped in a word search, or gobbled up by a quiz! I even heard there's a DRAGON around here somewhere.

Have you ever been to a new place that you weren't sure you'd like, but ended up loving?

Ohh, I wish I could go there. Maybe someday I'll pack my tiny bags and see what the rest of this book is all about.

Thanks for sharing with me. Now could you turn the page, please? That was so much excitement I think I need a nap.

YOUR MISSION

SHOULD YOU CHOOSE TO ACCEPT IT:

DEFEAT THE GREAT AND TERRIBLE WORRY DRAGON

STEP 1: DECORATE YOUR CAPE!

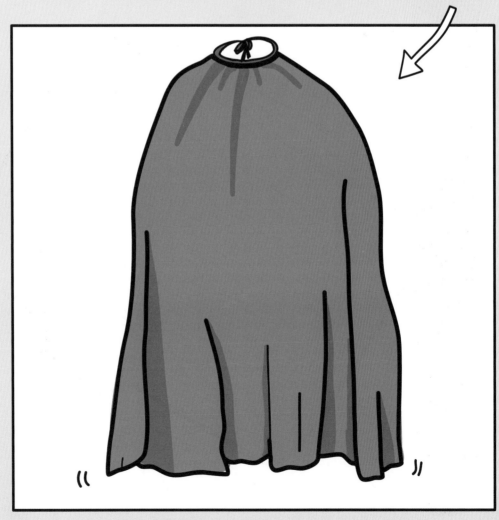

STEP 2: FILL YOUR BRIEFCASE WITH SECRET DRAGON-DEFEATING TOOLS

STEP 3: DEFEAT THE GREAT AND TERRIBLE DRAGON

DRAW *the* **THIRSTY CREATURE DRINKING** *this* **ENORMOUS DRINK**

Sometimes when we feel anxious, all we need is a big glass of water!

UNSCRAMBLE the EASY FIXES

Sometimes a bad feeling comes from your body needing something it's not getting . . . in which case the solution might be really, really simple. Next time you start feeling anxious, run through this checklist, then unscramble the easy solution you can try.

Am I hungry? Solution ⟶ TEA!

___ ___ ___ ___

Am I tired? Solution ⟶ NPA!

___ ___ ___

Am I thirsty? Solution ⟶ NRKDI!

___ ___ ___ ___ ___

Am I restless? Solution ⟶ RCEESXIE!

___ ___ ___ ___ ___ ___ ___ ___

Am I nervous? Solution ⟶ ARTBEHE!

___ ___ ___ ___ ___ ___ ___

Like I always say, if you're thirsty, try a cold nrkdi!

STUFF LITERALLY EVERYBODY DOES

Everybody poops: We know this. But there are lots of other things that everybody (yes, everybody!) does also.

Pick nose
Mess up
Feel left out

Fart
Trip
Swallow gum*

Worry
Feel dumb

```
D Z F A R T Z T Z T Z Z
U J M M N D R W E U C M
W H Y N B I M E T O J I
X S Y W P G S S F T R Q
J J M G O O Z M I F R R
H U F C N R N R M E A X
S B W K P G R A E L L A
A A C X T L S Y S L U Z
U I P E S T S O S E P P
P C R N A C F H U E J Z
B M U D L E E F P F S O
S W A L L O W G U M A S
```

*Don't do this; it will stay in your body for seven years.**

**This is not true. But still don't do this.

GRATITUDE LIST

Taking time to recognize the good stuff in your life can help you feel better, improve your health, and build strong relationships. The next time you're upset, try writing down a few things that make you happy. It just might work!

Today, I'm grateful for: _____
_____
_____

I'm also grateful for:

This person, who helped me when they didn't have to:
_____
_____

This person, who I had the opportunity to help: _____
_____
_____

This thing about my home: _____
_____
_____

This thing about my family: _____
_____
_____

This thing about myself: _____
_____
_____

YOU GET A PARTY

Hey, you! You're doing GREAT. So great, in fact, that you get a party. Decorate the scene for an epic celebration, and then add whomever you'd like to invite!

COLOR AND CUT OUT THESE DECORATIONS TO ADD TO THE OPPOSITE PAGE, OR MAKE YOUR OWN!

Balloons

So many balloons

Party banner, hello

Caaaaaaake

Confetti

Presents!

Some of your very best friends

TAKE A MINUTE
AND SOAK IN THIS
COLOR! DID YOU
KNOW BLUE CAN
MAKE YOU FEEL
CALM?

PEOPLE (AND PETS) WHO PROBABLY HAVE ANXIETY, TOO!

Fill in the blanks with the missing letters to reveal the answers!

MAI_PER _ _ _
S N O L

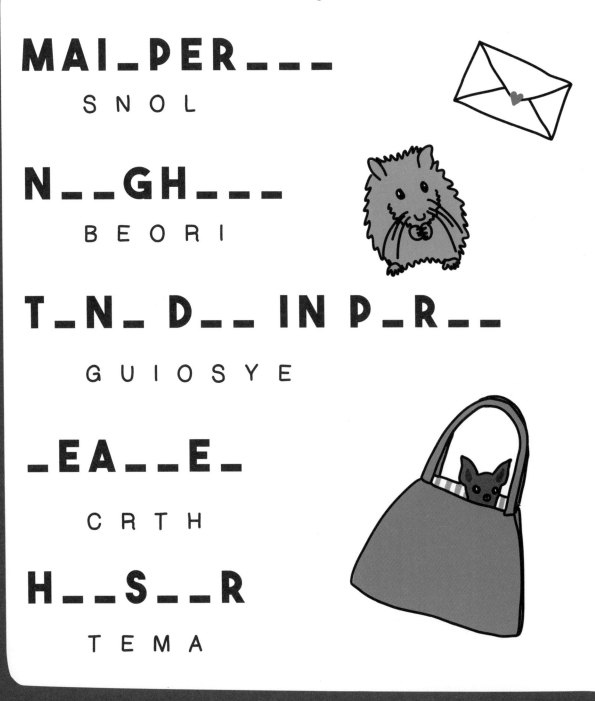

N_ _GH_ _ _
B E O R I

T_N_ D_ _ IN P_R_ _
G U I O S Y E

_EA_ _E_
C R T H

H_ _S_ _R
T E M A

ANIMAL FACTS TO MAKE YOU HAPPY

The back slime on a certain species of frog literally makes the flu virus explode. And removing it doesn't even hurt the frog!

Color us in!

When rabbits get really happy, they start to jump around in a specific way that is referred to as a "binky."

In 1966, the World Cup trophy was stolen. A dog named Pickles found it.

Cows have best friends.

Cats bring home dead animals because they're worried that their owners aren't good enough hunters to feed themselves.

Thousands of new trees are planted every year because squirrels forget where they buried their acorns.

There is a type of penguin that proposes to its chosen life partner with a pebble.

A 100-year-old tortoise named Diego single-handedly saved his species from extinction by fathering 800 tortoise babies.

There is a type of sea cucumber called "Donkey Dung." It looks exactly how you think it looks.

Rats laugh when you tickle them.

Scotland's national animal is the unicorn.

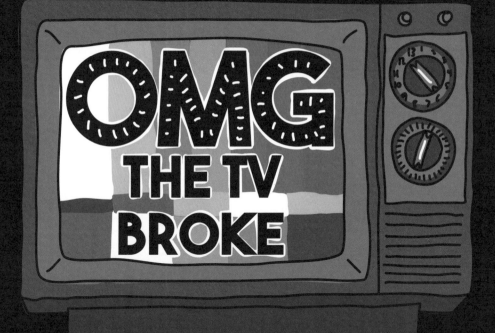

When suddenly deprived of screens, some of us

find ourselves wondering whether all joy has been

sucked out of the world via a WiFi-free black

hole. Sometimes our bored brains give us day-

dreams about riding on cloud dragons (fun!), but

other times they start whipping themselves up

into worry-tornados of anxiety (extremely un-fun)

SOLUTION:

Do something. Anything! Seriously, an-y-thing. Just trying something new often has the power to actually change how you feel for the better.

DECORATE THIS GINGERBREAD PERSON

Can I eat the gingerbread person when you're done?

WRITE A POEM ABOUT TOES

...and decorate these puppies!

GIVE THESE CATERPILLARS FUNNY NAMES

GIVE YOURSELF A HAIRSTYLE THAT YOU WOULD NEVER ACTUALLY GET IN A MILLION ZILLION YEARS.

draw said hairdo here

COLOR IN THIS UGLY (YET AWESOME) HOLIDAY SWEATER

FIX THE TV

PUT ON YOUR FAVORITE SONG
(THIS ONE: _____)
AND DANCE IT OUT

DESIGN YOUR PERSONAL LOGO

COOL FACTS TO THINK ABOUT WHEN YOU'RE

DAYDREAMING

In 2017, a group of high school students in Boca Raton, Florida, started a club to make sure that no one had to eat lunch alone.

Honey never goes bad. If you happen to have 3,000-year-old honey lying around, you can totally eat it.

The word SWIMS is still SWIMS if you turn it upside-down. (You have to use uppercase letters, though.)

Every day, we take about 22,000 breaths.

In the Indian village of Piplantri, residents plant 111 trees every time a baby girl is born.

When you snap your fingers, your thumb doesn't make a sound. What you're hearing in the "snap" is the sound of your middle finger hitting your palm.

Bug spray doesn't actually repel mosquitoes . . . it makes you smell different to them, making it hard for them to recognize you as dinner.

The largest pizza ever made was over 13,500 square feet.

"Huh?" is the closest thing humans have to a universal word: It's understood in almost every language on the planet.

When you were born, there was a moment when you were the youngest person in the universe.

Go outside and look up. What do you see in the clouds? Draw it here:

what really matters

blanket forts

grandparents

finding a person you really like (most of the time)

naps !!! zzz

books

dreams

fireflies

fixing things that are broken

if ~~people~~ you think you're super cool

practicing

resilience

sticking up for people when they can't stick up for themselves

cozy pajamas

baby bunnies

this person!

this place:

this random thing only I understand!

magic

your doodles
go here!

STOP, SLOW, OR GO?

Some skills—like learning to drive!—take practice, and some might already be in your comfort zone. Color in the traffic sign that matches how you feel about each of the below.

Raising my hand in class

Speaking up when I know something's wrong

Going to a party

Meeting new people

Performing onstage

Trying out for a team sport

Confronting a bully

Asking for help

Showing my feelings

STOP

SLOW

GO!

Learning a new skill

Being alone

Taking a test

EVERYBODY GETS ANXIOUS SOMETIMES!

Ask four people you know to draw something that makes them anxious.

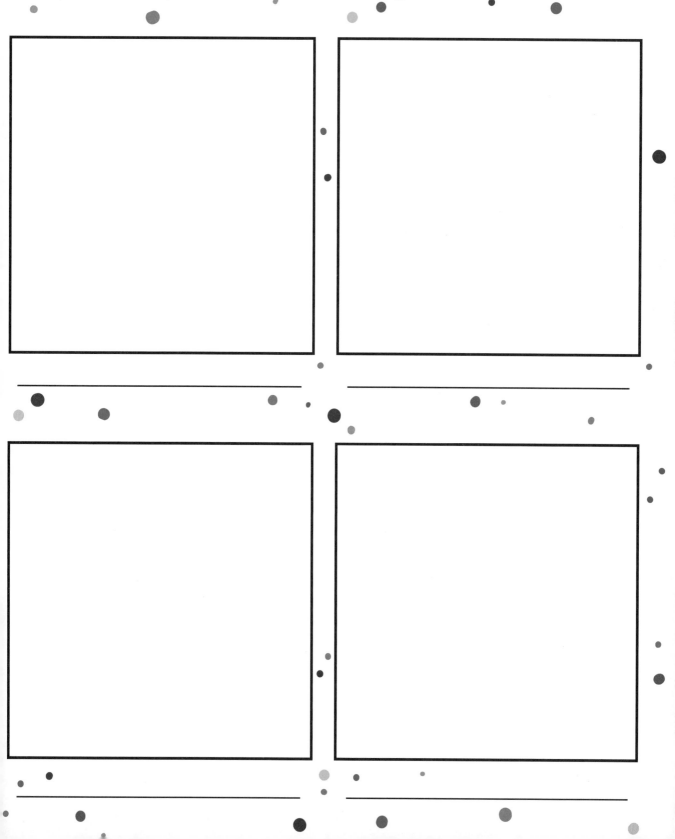

SCRIBBLE OVER THE LITTLE MONSTERS YOU ARE NOT GOING TO STRESS ABOUT

This little monster making fun of you for wearing socks that are the wrong height (according to said little monster, who is apparently an International Sock Expert)

This little monster who thinks you should hide your emotions

This little monster who has exactly one word in its vocabulary

This little monster who thinks it's OK to judge someone else's personal choices

DRAW FIVE THINGS THAT MAKE YOU FEEL SAFE

. . . and add them to this lockbox for safekeeping.

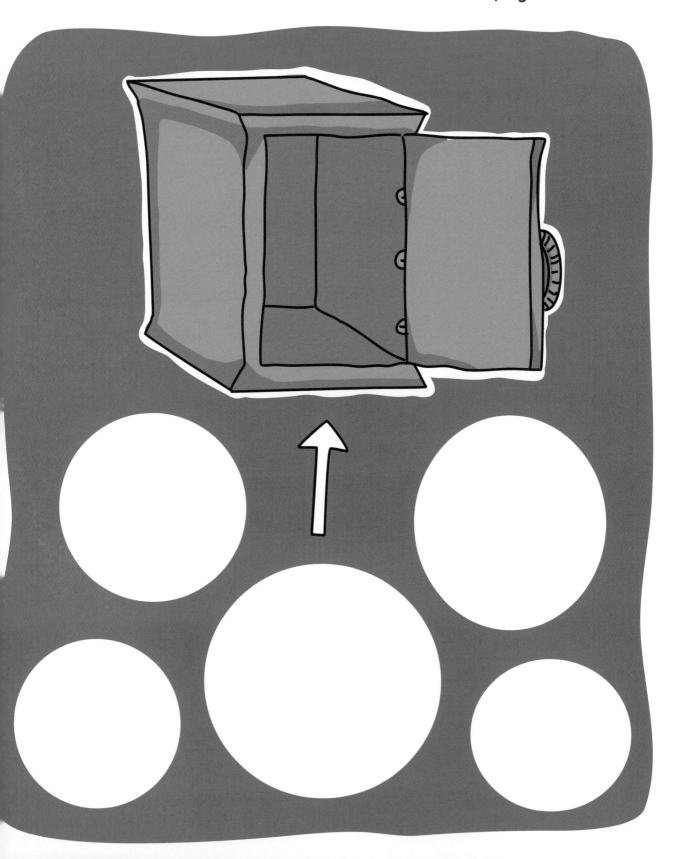

HOW TO:
CALM DOWN WHEN YOU'RE FREAKING OUT

Have you ever been in a super-stressful situation (say, you just erased your entire history project that is due in literally 15 minutes, and now your computer is broken because, okay, maybe you threw it out the window?) and then someone told you to "just calm down"? This is unhelpful advice, because it is annoying.

WHAT TO DO INSTEAD:

Isn't science cool?!

BREATHE

It's the actual scientific way to trick your body into thinking everything is awesome, even if what is happening is that you're being chased by a gorilla. This is because deep breathing increases the flow of oxygen to your brain and slows down your heart rate, tricking your body into feeling calm.

RUN COLD WATER OVER YOUR WRISTS

Your wrists have major arteries in them, so cooling them will help distribute that cool blood through the rest of your body—and you'll literally chill out! (Sorry, bad joke.)

EAT A HANDFUL OF SOMETHING CRUNCHY

When you're anxious, your jaw starts acting like a rottweiler with a steak— and chewing helps relax it.

SMELL SOME COFFEE

Grab your grown-up's mug and give it a big sniff. Scientists have discovered that this calms down rats . . . so maybe it'll work for you, too!

COUNT BACKWARD FROM 100

This is harder than you think, and forces your brain to concentrate on something other than what's bugging you.

EAT A SQUARE OF CHOCOLATE

Chocolate increases your serotonin levels (the stuff in your brain that makes you feel good). It's also delicious.

THE ANXIETY TOOLBOX

When you start feeling anxious, it's super helpful to know what tools you have at hand. Color in the tools below and then write down your own in the journaling section underneath!

Sleep mask (zzzz)

Carrots (so crunchy!)

This book (obviously)

A plan

Music you love to dance to

Cup of tea (decaf, please)

Cozy pillow

Running shoes—exercise is a mood booster!

What's in your anxiety toolbox?

_____

_____

_____

NOPE, NOT HELPFUL

When people (adults, mostly) notice that you're upset, they might want to give you advice. Sometimes, though, that advice can feel really unhelpful. Cross out all the phrases you've had someone say to you (ugh), then flip the page for what they probably should have said instead.

These are the WORST

Calm down
It's all in your head
Just get over it
You're overreacting
It's not a big deal
Don't be such a baby
Why are you like this?
Just stop worrying so much!
A lot of people have it worse, you know
Sings "If you're happy and you know it clap your hands!"

(I hate this one the most: _____ .)

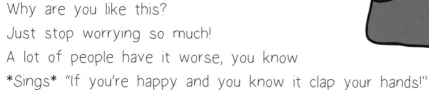

FLIP PAGE

Circle all the things you'd like someone to say to you next time you're feeling anxious.

"I hear what you're saying. Is there anything I can do to help?"
"I'm always here if you want to talk."
"Do you want advice, or would you rather I just listen?"
"What you're feeling isn't silly."
"Let's figure this out together."
"I love you, no matter what."
Nothing. Just sitting together helps.

Sandwiches

WE ALL MAKE MISTAKES

Lots of them!

Check off the mistakes you (along with, ya know, most other people on planet Earth) have made:

Left the oven on

Forgot about Easter

Said wrong answer in class

Yelled at pet hamster

- ☐ Told a lie
- ☐ Cheated
- ☐ Said something to a friend I wish I hadn't
- ☐ Didn't try as hard as I could have
- ☐ Quit because something got too difficult
- ☐ Forgot to do something really important
- ☐ Cared too much about what someone else thought
- ☐ Gave in to peer pressure
- ☐ Scored a point for the other team
- ☐ Forgot the rules
- ☐ Was mean to someone for no reason
- ☐ Didn't respect someone else's point of view
- ☐ Overreacted to something that wasn't actually a big deal
- ☐ Disappointed someone I care about
- ☐ Let myself down

The good news: mistakes aren't just unavoidable . . . they're important! If you're not making mistakes, you're not trying new things—and not trying new things is the biggest mistake of them all.

HOORAY FOR MISTAKES

Just listen to what these wise people have to say! And if you need a reminder, cut out your favorite quotes below and tape them up somewhere special.

WHAT'S ON YOUR PLATE?

Write down everything you have to deal with today on this plate.

Now let's take a few things off.

Put ✗ s through things that are really other people's responsibilities.

Scribble out things that you can't control.

Put a wavy line through things that don't need to get done right now. ~~

Whew! Now, that is a to-do list you can handle.

THINGS THAT DO NOT HELP

Nerves feeling jangly? Step away from the Snickers. Sweet treats are fine once in a while, but if you're getting the jitters, a steady stream of sweets won't help!

SUPPORT SYSTEM HALL OF FAME

Who always makes you feel stronger? Draw their portraits on this fancy wall, and write how they support you in the corresponding blob.

Especially this person ♡

THINGS I'M NOT AFRAID OF

Take a moment to feel proud of some things that you used to be scared of . . . until you overcame those fears. Well done! (And just for fun, list a few things that have never scared you.)

I USED TO BE AFRAID OF:

I WAS NEVER AFRAID OF:

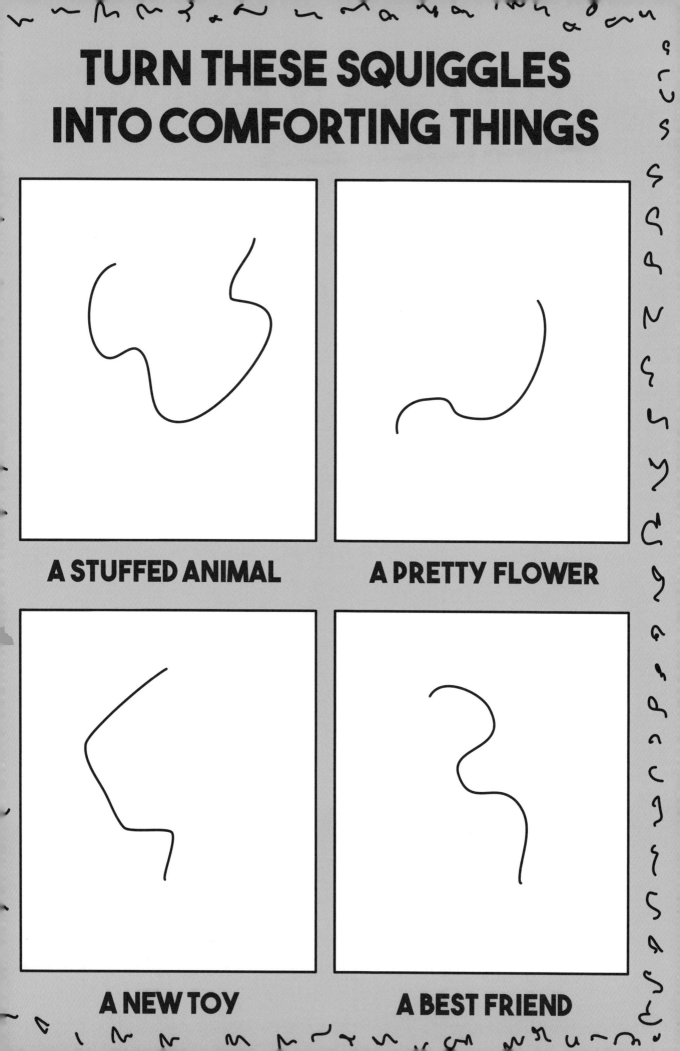

WRITE A SCARY ENDING TO THIS STORY

One afternoon, I decided to take my dog, Sadie, for a walk in the woods. After a while, I realized I was lost, and the sun was going down.

It was getting darker and darker, and after a while I realized that we weren't any closer to home than we'd been when we started. We turned around right away—I should have been home two hours ago! Over there was the same scraggly bush we'd passed three times! Even Sadie was starting to whine. She must have been hungry. I was, too.

The clouds were so thick, I couldn't even see any stars. I could barely see anything. And then, all of a sudden, I saw it, right there in a bush.

_____

_____

_____

_____

_____

_____

_____

Yikes, that was scary. Thank goodness it's just a story!

NOW WRITE A HAPPIER ENDING

_____

_____

_____

_____

_____

_____

_____

_____

Happy endings
should always
include ice cream

Which ending do you think would be more likely to happen?

TOP 5 THINGS I'M MOST PROUD OF

Grew hair down to butt

1.

2.

3.

4.

5.

REPORT CARD			
	Q1	Q2	Q3
Science	A-	A	
History	B+	A-	
Gym	C+	B	
Reading	B-	B+	

Better grades

Read 10 books last summer

Learned Swahili

Jambo!

Joined marching band

TAKE A BOW

Draw yourself showing off a super-cool talent in front of this adoring audience!

Giant person! It's you! I made it off my page! I only got a little bit sweaty.
Want to know how I did it?! Every time I started getting super nervous, I used something called . . .
SHUSH'S
MINDFULNESS TECHNIQUE FOR BEING LESS NERVOUS AND SWEATY

THE WORRY SHELF

Write down five things that have been bugging you lately.

1. _____
2. _____
3. _____
4. _____
5. _____

Circle the ones you can do something about and think about what you're going to do about them.

Put a box around the ones you can't do anything about—at least not right now.

Now put those worries on the shelf—there's a spot for them right here! You can take them down later, if and when you're ready.

CIRCLE ALL THE THINGS YOU NEED TO APOLOGIZE FOR, AND X OUT THE ONES YOU DON'T

Hurting someone else (on purpose or accidentally)

Needing some time for yourself

Who you like

Who you love

Saying no when you're uncomfortable

Someone bumping into you on the street

Asking someone to fix a mistake they made

Asking for help

Not knowing the answer

Being imperfect

Being awesome

ANSWERS, AHOY!

The first item is the only one on this list you should say sorry for. NEVER apologize for being your imperfectly awesome self, K?

TOP 5 THINGS THAT MAKE ME FEEL CALM

Puzzles

Mom

1.

2.

3.

4.

5.

Well-loved friend

Hot bath

Swings

NOW GIVE YOURSELF THOSE THINGS

Draw a picture of yourself thinking about all those things that make you feel good.

SHOULD I ASK FOR HELP?

This is an easy quiz.

1. Do you feel like you might need help?   Yes   No

2. Do you feel like you might want help?   Yes   No

If you answered "Yes" to either of the above questions: Ask for help! It takes real bravery, but it's the smartest thing you can do.

Circle the people who you can ask for help if you need it.

Mom

Dad

Best friend

Grandparent

Adult friend I trust (This one: _____)

Adult family member I trust (This one: _____)

Neighbor

Teacher

School counselor

Doctor

Also these people!

REAL SUPERHEROES ASK FOR HELP

Draw you and your super helper below. Don't forget to decorate your costumes!

MASTERFULLY NAVIGATE THE TRICKY SITUATION!

Avoid people who tell you to "just relax"! Distracting TV shows! Chores you forgot about! Giving up and going to bed!

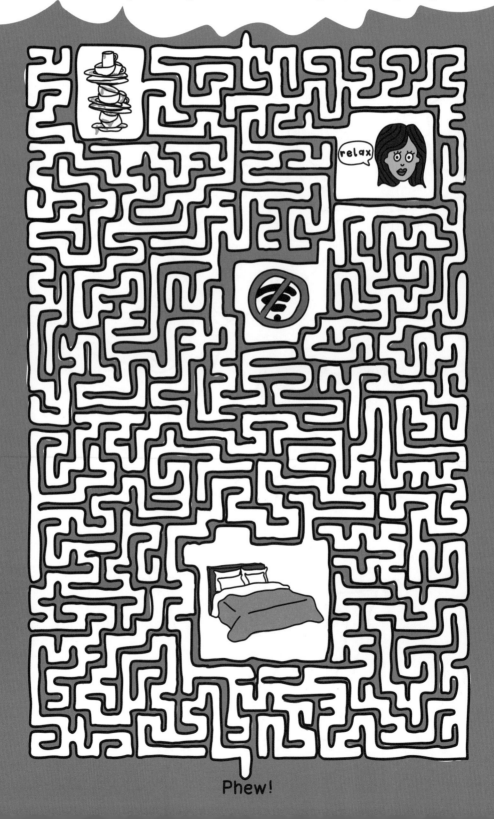

Phew!

GIVE YOURSELF AN AWARD

Decorate this with your name in super-fancy writing.

What's it for?!?!?!

_____

_____

HOW TO: MAKE YOUR OWN HAPPY PLACE

Pssst: Your happy place doesn't have to be an actual "place" . . . you can make one up in your mind!

When you picture being somewhere relaxing, where are you?
- ☐ The beach
- ☐ Somewhere snowy
- ☐ The woods
- ☐ A park or playground
- ☐ A field
- ☐ My bedroom at home

on the swings?

palm trees, maybe?

Who else is there?
- ☐ My best friend
- ☐ My parents
- ☐ My pet
- ☐ This fuzzy little guy →
- ☐ Nobody but me!

...in case you need a reference for drawing me...

um, no →

What do you hear?

_____

What do you smell?

_____

What do you taste?

_____

When you look around, what are a few wonderful things you see?

_____

_____

That sounds like the happiest place EVER. *and it's all yours* ♥

DRAW YOURSELF IN YOUR OFFICIAL HAPPY PLACE

And remember, anytime you want to come back here, all you have to do is close your eyes.

THE
END